Dear Sir, I Intend to Burn Your Book

WITHDRAWN

Dear Sir, I Intend to Burn Your Book

An Anatomy of a Book Burning

LAWRENCE HILL

CANADIAN LITERATURE CENTRE
CENTRE DE LITTÉRATURE CANADIENNE

CANADIAN LITERATURE CENTRE/
CENTRE DE LITTÉRATURE CANADIENNE

THE UNIVERSITY OF ALBERTA PRESS

Published by

The University of Alberta Press
Ring House 2
Edmonton, Alberta, Canada T6G 2E1
www.uap.ualberta.ca

and

Canadian Literature Centre /
Centre de littérature canadienne
3–5 Humanities Centre
University of Alberta
Edmonton, Alberta, Canada T6G 2E5
www. www.arts.ualberta.ca/clc

LIBRARY AND ARCHIVES CANADA
CATALOGUING IN PUBLICATION

Hill, Lawrence, 1957–

    Dear Sir, I intend to burn your book :
an anatomy of a book burning /
Lawrence Hill.

(Henry Kreisel memorial lecture series)
Co-published by Canadian Literature
Centre/Centre de littérature canadienne.
Issued also in electronic formats.
ISBN 978-0-88864-679-8

    1. Censorship. 2. Books and reading–
Political aspects. 3. Intellectual freedom.
4. Freedom of expression. I. University
of Alberta. Canadian Literature Centre
II. Title. III. Series: Henry Kreisel lecture
series

Z659.H55 2013   323.44   C2013-901210-9

First edition, first printing, 2013.
Printed and bound in Canada by
Houghton Boston Printers,
Saskatoon, Saskatchewan.
Copyediting by Peter Midgley.

The University of Alberta Press is
committed to protecting our natural
environment. As part of our efforts,
this book is printed on Enviro Paper: it
contains 100% post-consumer recycled
fibres and is acid- and chlorine-free.

The Canadian Literature Centre
acknowledges the support of the Alberta
Foundation for the Arts for the Henry
Kreisel Lecture delivered by Lawrence Hill
in April 2012 at the University of Alberta.

The University of Alberta Press gratefully
acknowledges the support received for
its publishing program from The Canada
Council for the Arts. The University of
Alberta Press also gratefully acknowledges
the financial support of the Government
of Canada through the Canada Book
Fund (CBF) and the Government of
Alberta through the Alberta Multimedia
Development Fund (AMDF) for its
publishing activities.

Canada

Canada Council   Conseil des Arts
for the Arts   du Canada

Alberta
Government

Foreword

PERHAPS ABOVE ALL THE OTHER ACTIVITIES run by
the Canadian Literature Centre, the Henry Kreisel Lecture
Series realizes most fully the CLC's mission to bring together
in a meaningful way author, reader, student and professor of
Canadian writing in English and French. The CLC was estab-
lished in 2006, thanks to a leadership gift by Edmonton's
noted bibliophile, Dr. Eric Schloss. Dr. Schloss' continued
support attests both to his generosity and to his great
passion for the literatures of this country.

The Kreisel Lectures are delivered by such passion-
ately engaged and major award-winning authors as Joseph
Boyden, Wayne Johnston, Dany Laferrière, Eden Robinson,
Annabel Lyon, and most recently, Lawrence Hill. They
foster an open and inclusive forum for critical thinking
about Canadian writing certainly, but also about social and

cultural issues that vividly and closely touch us personally and, more widely, as citizens. Take the fine points about
social oppression, cultural identities, and sense of place
treated by Boyden, or the sometimes tumultuous encounter
of history and fiction experienced by Johnston. Consider
both the pains of exile and the joys of migrancy brought
forth by Laferrière, or the personal and communal ethics
of storytelling that Robinson tackles. The ancient past and
the contemporary moment come together through Lyon's
discussion of the creative process of historical fiction. And
here in these remarkable pages, Hill makes an appealingly
personal and politically convincing plea for the urgent need
of an informed conversation about book censorship.

The lectures in this Kreisel Series confront the important
questions of our time, those that touch us deeply as readers
and thinkers—as women and men, as Canadians, and as
contemporary social individuals. In the spirit of true and
honest dialogue, they do so with the thoughtfulness and
depth as well as the humour and elegance which all charac-
terize, in one way or another, the work of the six incredibly
talented writers featured in the Kreisel Series so far.

These public lectures set out to honour Professor
Henry Kreisel's legacy in an annual public forum. Author,
University Professor and Officer of the Order of Canada,
Henry Kreisel was born in Vienna into a Jewish family in
1922. He left his homeland for England in 1938 and was
interned in Canada for eighteen months during the Second
World War. After studying at the University of Toronto, he
began teaching in 1947 at the University of Alberta, and

served as Chair of English from 1961 until 1970. He served as Vice-President (Academic) from 1970 to 1975, and was named University Professor in 1975, the highest scholarly award bestowed on its faculty members by the University of Alberta. Professor Kreisel was an inspiring and beloved teacher who taught generations of students to love literature and was one of the first people to bring the experience of the immigrant to modern Canadian literature. He died in Edmonton in 1991. His works include two novels, *The Rich Man* (1948) and *The Betrayal* (1964), and a collection of short stories, *The Almost Meeting* (1981). His internment diary, alongside critical essays on his writing, appears in *Another Country: Writings By and About Henry Kreisel* (1985).

The generosity of Professor Kreisel's teaching at the University of Alberta and his influence on modern Canadian literature profoundly inspire the CLC in its public outreach, research pursuits, and continued commitment to the ever-growing richness and diversity of Canada's literatures. The Centre embraces Henry Kreisel's no less than pioneering focus on the knowledge of one's own literatures. It embraces the understanding of the complicated and difficult world which informs Canadian writings and which may well be bettered and transformed by them.

MARIE CARRIÈRE
Director, Canadian Literature Centre
Edmonton, February 2013

Liminaire

PEUT-ÊTRE PLUS QUE TOUTE AUTRE ACTIVITÉ menée
par le Centre de littérature canadienne, les conférences
Kreisel réalisent intégralement la mission du CLC de
rassembler de manière constructive auteur, lecteur, étudiant
et professeur de littérature canadienne d'expression
anglaise et française. Le CLC a été créé en 2006 grâce au don
directeur du bibliophile illustre edmontonien, le docteur
Eric Schloss. L'appui continu du docteur Schloss témoigne
de sa générosité et sa grande passion vis-à-vis des littératures
du Canada.

Les conférenciers Kreisel comptent parmi eux Joseph
Boyden, Wayne Johnson, Dany Laferrière, Eden Robinson,
Annabel Lyon et plus récemment Lawrence Hill, tous des
auteurs passionnément engagés et lauréats de prix impor-
tants. Les conférences favorisent un forum ouvert et inclusif

pour la pensée critique, au sujet certes des écrits du Canada, mais aussi des questions sociales et culturelles qui nous saisissent comme individus et comme citoyens plus largement. Pensons aux fines observations de Boyden sur l'oppression sociale, les identités culturelles et l'idée du lieu, ou à la rencontre parfois tumultueuse de l'histoire et la fiction vécue par Johnston. Tenons compte des épreuves de l'exil et des joies de la migrance avancées par Laferrière, ou de l'éthique personnelle et communautaire de la narration traitée par Robinson. L'antiquité et le contemporain se réunissent dans la communication de Lyon au sujet du mode créatif de la fiction historique. Et dans les pages remarquables qui suivent, il est fort intéressant de lire le plaidoyer politique et personnel de Hill pour le besoin urgent d'une conversation informée sur la censure des livres.

Les conférences de la collection Kreisel abordent les questions importantes de notre époque, celles qui nous concernent profondément dans nos lectures et nos pensées—en tant que Canadiennes et Canadiens et en tant qu'individus dans une société contemporaine. Dans une intention de dialogue véritable et honnête, ces conférences reflètent l'ardeur et la profondeur intellectuelles ainsi que l'humour et l'élégance de l'œuvre de ces six auteurs extrêmement doués et présentés jusqu'ici par la collection Kreisel.

Ces conférences publiques se consacrent annuellement à perpétuer la mémoire du Professeur Henry Kreisel. Auteur, professeur universitaire et Officier de l'Ordre du Canada, Henry Kreisel est né à Vienne d'une famille juive en 1922. En 1938, il a quitté son pays natal pour l'Angleterre et a été interné pendant dix-huit mois, au Canada, lors de la Deuxième Guerre mondiale. Après ses études à l'Université de Toronto, il devint professeur à l'Université de l'Alberta en 1947, et à partir de 1961 jusqu'à 1970, il a dirigé le département d'anglais. De 1970 à 1975, il a été vice-recteur (universitaire), et a été nommé professeur hors rang en 1975, la plus haute distinction scientifique décernée par l'Université de l'Alberta à un membre de son professorat. Professeur adoré, il a transmis l'amour de la littérature à plusieurs générations d'étudiants, et il a été parmi les premiers écrivains modernes du Canada à aborder l'expérience immigrante. Il est décédé à Edmonton en 1991. Son œuvre comprend les romans, *The Rich Man* (1948) et *The Betrayal* (1964), et un recueil de nouvelles intitulé *The Almost Meeting* (1981). Son journal d'internement, accompagné d'articles critiques sur ses écrits, paraît dans *Another Country: Writings By and About Henry Kreisel* (1985).

La générosité de l'enseignement du Professeur Kreisel et son influence sur la littérature moderne du Canada inspirent profondément le travail public et scientifique du CLC et son engagement à l'égard de la diversité et la qualité remarquables des écrits du Canada. Le Centre adhère à l'importance qu'accordait de façon inaugurale Henry Kreisel à la connaissance des littératures de son propre pays. Enfin, le CLC poursuit la compréhension d'un monde compliqué et difficile qui détermine les littératures canadiennes et qui peut bien se voir amélioré et transformé par elles.

MARIE CARRIÈRE

Directrice, Centre de littérature canadienne

Edmonton, février 2013

Introduction

THE HENRY KREISEL MEMORIAL LECTURE SERIES has
evolved into a much-anticipated event, one of the wonderful
things that the Canadian Literature Centre does under the
leadership of Professor Marie Carrière—and I think we
often forget that she is not a full-time fundraiser and event
planner. She is in fact a professor of Canadian Literature, so
our thanks to her.

Our thanks as well to the sponsors of this event, Eric and
Elexis Schloss. Those of you who know Eric will confirm
that he tells *terrible* jokes (one about a blind guy eating
matzo on a park bench comes to mind), but Elexis loves him
and we do too because he loves books and his enthusiasm
animates not only the CLC but also Edmonton's Litfest, of
which he is a board member.

Many of us first became aware of Lawrence Hill through his fabulous *The Book of Negroes*—it won the Commonwealth Writers Prize, the Roger's Writer's Trust Prize, and CBC's Canada Reads; internationally it was nominated for the IMPAC award.

The Book of Negroes sold more than 600,000 copies—over half a million—in Canada alone, where sales of 5,000 constitute a bestseller. Astonishing. There isn't even a vampire in it. This was popular fiction that was the reverse of escapist entertainment.

So, one wonders, who is this new guy?

It turns out he's not new—we just hadn't been paying attention. His parents came to Canada from Washington, DC the day after they were married. He was born in Newmarket, Ontario. His father was black, his mother white, and they were both human rights activists. In his Commonwealth Prize acceptance speech, Lawrence Hill talks about how when they were growing up he was not allowed to consume Aunt Jemima pancake syrup because of the stereotyped image on the label.

He worked as a reporter for the *Globe and Mail* in Toronto and for the *Winnipeg Free Press*, but he [like local Edmonton author Todd Babiak] wanted to write fiction, not newspaper stories, and so he quit his job and at the age of 27 moved to Spain, where he wrote for hours every day on a typewriter that he borrowed from a nearby typing school. He returned with short stories, some of which went on to be published, and then began to write his first novel, *Some Great Thing*, which was published by Turnstone Press in Winnipeg in

1992. After that, he was picked up by HarperCollins, which publishes his work now.

He went on to write two more novels, *Any Known Blood* (1997) and four non-fiction books:

> *Trials and Triumphs: The Story of African-Canadians* (1993);
> *Women of Vision: The Story of the Canadian Negro Women's Association* (1996);
> *Black Berry, Sweet Juice: On Being Black and White in Canada* (2001); and
> *The Deserter's Tale: The Story of an Ordinary Soldier Who Walked Away from the War in Iraq,* with Joshua Key.

He wrote the screenplay for *Seeking Salvation*, a 90-minute documentary about the Black church in Canada, which won the American Wilbur Award for best national television documentary in 2005.

In 2010, he was awarded the Bob Edwards Award from the Alberta Theatre Projects in Calgary, which "recognizes a literary figure who has demonstrated outstanding curiosity and respect for freedom of expression." Most recently, The Writers' Union of Canada awarded him the 2012 Freedom to Read Award.

Lawrence Hill is so famous he was interviewed by George Strombolopolous. In the interview, he talks about meeting the Queen of England, and how her hand started moving toward the silver button that calls security when she's bored with you…and so, like Scheherazade in the Arabian Nights, he kept trying to be more and more interesting.

And he talks about how, after two novels—*Some Great Thing* and *Any Known Blood*—in which the main character is a man, it was "scary" to write from the point of view of a woman. He says "I got into the voice with a whole lot of cross-dressing"…and then more seriously says he thought about writing from the perspective of his daughter.

He's a funny guy, but his writing has an edge.

Ten years ago I had a very bright young woman in my class, an excellent writer, and very exotic looking (and "exotic" is hardly a neutral term). I asked her, "Where are you from?"

She said, "Canada." And then she elaborated: "My parents are from Malaysia—my mother was from the Philippines, my father from India, my grandfather was Portuguese, my grandmother from China, what was Formosa.'"

Then earlier this month while reading Lawrence Hill's non-fiction book *Black Berry, Sweet Juice* I encountered his essay, "The Question."

It turns out I had been asking The Question. He gives us the dialogue that begins with The Question, "Where are you from?" which is, he says, code for "What is your race."

He replies, "Canada," which is code for "Screw Off."

Which forces his interrogator into more pointed questions, such as "But your place of origin? Your parents?" still avoiding the topic of race.

Reading Hill, my exchange with my student came back to me—not an exchange, I now saw, but an interrogation, one that, I now realized, she had endured hundreds of times before. She was kind enough to skip the intervening steps and answer the question I was really asking.

The exchange with my student illustrates why we need writers like Lawrence Hill. His work takes us into the complexity of race, with humour, sensitivity, and love. It doesn't lecture; it dramatizes, immersing us in the situations of his characters, revealing to us our often-unexamined assumptions.

We in this country—at least those of us of my generation—don't know how to talk about race. We're scared to even mention the word. However, the landscape is changing. As we become a more global economy and we create a more global community, race doesn't fit into neat boxes any more. Not that it ever did.

But the account of race relations in Canada has more often been consigned to the dusty boxes of archives, where characters are just lines in a ledger; Lawrence Hill digs into our past, giving life and form to the spare record. Talking about the challenges of writing historical fiction, he says, "The difficulty is respecting the broad lines of history, stamping the fresh face of fiction over the past, and being creative and lively at the same time....Part of my job as a novelist is to write the colour—and by that I mean human drama and struggle—back into history." Novels such as *The Book of Negroes* fuse the work of a scholar with the art of a novelist, bringing to life a history that my generation has largely ignored; and Hill's non-fiction raises questions, like "The Question," that rarely get asked.

Yet what makes it all work is the suppleness of Hill's prose. He has recently published in *The Walrus* one of the best prairie stories I've ever read—"Meet you at the Door," about a train operator in Saskatchewan. He captures the sense of space and distance in a way that would make W.O. Mitchell envious.

You can see that Lawrence Hill's vision encompasses both the global and the local. He says, "I love novels that are anchored in specific times and situations. This doesn't make them regional. This makes them real."[1]

TED BISHOP

Edmonton, February 2013

Dear Sir, I Intend to Burn Your Book

An Anatomy of a Book Burning

IN JUNE 2011, less than a month after launching the Dutch edition of my novel, *The Book of Negroes,* in The Netherlands, I received the most surprising email of my life. It is worth quoting verbatim:

Dear Sir Lawrence Hill,

We, descendants of enslaved in the former Dutch colony Suriname, want let you know that we do not accept a book with the title "The book of Negroes."
　　We struggle for a long time to let the word "nigger" disappears from Dutch language and now you set up your book of Negroes! A real shame!
　　That's why we make the decision to burn this book on the 22nd of June 2011.

Maybe you do not know, but June is the month before the 1st of July, the day that we remember the abolition from the Dutch, who put our ancestors in slavery.

Sincerely,
ROY GROENBERG,
Chairman Foundation Honor and Restore Victims of Slavery in Suriname

Attached to the email was a handwritten poster saying, in Dutch, "Summons to Afro-Surinamese-Dutch people to come to Bookburning in Oosterpark near the monument."

I wrote a reply that, in retrospect, seems outrageously Canadian in its politeness and tact. Here's what I said:

Dear Mr. Groenberg,

I am very sorry to hear of your plans to burn my book.

Are you aware of the historical origins of the title? It is a historical novel. "The Book of Negroes" is the name of a British military ledger, that documented the exodus of 3,000 African Americans from New York City to Nova Scotia, Canada at the end of the American Revolutionary War. It is a very important genealogical document, as it provides a great deal of biographical information about the Blacks who migrated from the USA to Canada in 1783. The original copy of this document is kept in the National Archives in the UK. The document is central to my novel. My main character must have her name entered into

"The Book of Negroes" before she, like 3,000 other Blacks fleeing American slavery, is allowed to sail to Canada.

The use of the title, "The Book of Negroes" (or "Het Negerboek" in Dutch) has offered me the opportunity to explain this history, which is fascinating, important and troubling, to many thousands of readers in Canada, the UK, The Netherlands and elsewhere. I have found that when given the opportunity to see what I am doing in this book and with this title, readers understand that the title is not intended to be offensive, but that it is used historically, to shed light on a forgotten document and on a forgotten migration (that of thousands of Blacks from the USA to Canada in 1783).

Did you know that I gave a talk recently about this book, its historical origins, and the title, to the Surinamese group NiNsee in Amsterdam last month?

Before you proceed with your plans to burn my novel, would you like to have a conversation about this?

Thank you,
LAWRENCE HILL

As you may imagine, the conversation never took place. Mr. Groenberg went on to burn not the real book, but copies of the cover of my novel for Dutch TV cameras in the popular Oosterpark in Amsterdam, next to a monument commemorating the victims of Dutch slavery. I am not certain about the motivation for his actions. Perhaps his actions were inspired by a previous incident of book destruction in

Amsterdam. I don't know why Mr. Groenberg pulled back.
Maybe the burning of the covers sufficed for the photogra-
phers. From a comfortable chair on this side of the ocean, I
suppose that some might find the entire episode laughable.
It really shook me up. Obviously, I felt deeply troubled that
a work to which I had given five years of passion and attention and integrity should attract such a hateful act. To me,
the entire point of the novel was to offer dignity, depth and
dimensionality to a person whose very humanity would
have been assaulted as a slave. From my perspective, Mr.
Groenberg and I should have been on the same side of issues
having to do with the treatment and depiction of people in
the African Diaspora. My publisher felt ashamed to see the
book assailed in this manner and defended the book vigor-
ously. She received a death threat and decided not to attend
the book cover burning to see it for herself.

It wasn't the first time the title of my novel has encountered difficulties. Several months after it appeared in Canada
under the title *The Book of Negroes*, my American publisher
informed me right before going to the printer that it was
changing the name of the novel. Why? Because US bookstores were refusing to place advance orders for my novel
because the word "Negroes" was in the title. I was on book
tour in Germany at the time that I received this last-minute
email from my editor in Manhattan, and the most I could
negotiate was that I would be the one to come up with a
new title for the American edition. I had about 72 hours to
conjure up a new title, and found it with the assistance of
my then ten-year-old stepdaughter Eve Freedman—more

on her later—in a little hotel in the town of Greifswald in the former East Germany on the Baltic Sea. In the United States, and later in Australia and New Zealand, my novel was published under the title *Someone Knows My Name*.

It was a frustrating exercise. I didn't like having the title changed on me, but as time went on I came to appreciate that the word "Negroes" has become offensive in American culture—particularly in Black urban culture, where its meaning has evolved over time.

My father proudly called himself a Negro for most of his life. Indeed, when he was named Chair of the Ontario Human Rights Commission in 1973, the *Globe and Mail* ran a headline that said "Commission appoints Negro Chair." It was meant to be a polite headline, at the time. But that was 1973 and times have changed. These days, on the streets of urban America, calling a person a "Negro" implies that he or she is an inauthentic Black person with no self-pride and no self-respect. While I have been on book tours in the United States, over and over again African Americans have come up to me and said, "It's a good thing you changed the title of your book, because I would never have bought your book or come hear you speak if you had called it *The Book of Negroes* down here."

So, in joining J. K. Rowling and Alice Munro as just some of the many British and Canadian writers whose titles have been altered to suit the whims of American publishers, I eventually came to appreciate that there was a deep, simmering anger over the use of the word "Negro" in contemporary America. The word is far more explosive on the streets of Brooklyn, say, than it is in Edmonton. Try it out for yourself, if you don't believe me. Using it in Edmonton will probably earn you *The Look*, as if to say, "Have you not read the pages of a newspaper for 30 years?" If you use it in Brooklyn, be sure to travel with good health insurance.

The fact of the title change of my novel in certain markets, followed by the burning of the cover of *The Book of Negroes* in Amsterdam, led me to reflect more deeply on issues related to the historical injustices faced by racial, religious and other minorities, and the myriad ways that both victims and perpetrators of injustice have taken to burning, censoring and banning books historically and today.

It also led me to reflect on appropriate titles for future translations of the book. In Québec and in France, the title of *The Book of Negroes* has been translated as *Aminata*—the name of my protagonist. I, for one, insisted while the translation was being developed that there was no good literal translation for *The Book of Negroes*, and that however it came out, it would come out sounding flat and crass. After the problems in The Netherlands, a German publisher offered on the novel. I made sure that publisher was aware of the problems that had arisen in The Netherlands, and I believe that the decision has been made to base the German title on the American, *Someone Knows My Name*.

There is something particularly odious about burning a book, or a pile of books. The action aims not just to remove the offending article from the hands of readers, but to silence and intimidate writers, publishers and booksellers. It suggests that they too will be burned if they do not heed the message. The act seems to say: "You will not be tolerated. Your ideas will not be discussed. We must protect society from your toxic mind, and so we are lighting this bonfire."

As early as the year 1141, the Talmud was burned in Paris on charges of blasphemy. The leaders of the Spanish Inquisition burned books. Nazis burned books. And did they ever. Many books have been written on the subject of banning and censoring books, but one that can be recommended for its clarity and brevity is *Forbidden Fruit: Banned, Censored, and Challenged Books from Dante to Harry Potter*, by Pearce Carefoote.[2] *Forbidden Fruit* notes that in Berlin's Opernplatz on May 10, 1933, Nazis burned 25,000 volumes by Jewish and other ostensibly seditious writers. Tossed into the raging fires were, among others, works by Karl Marx, Sigmund Freud, Helen Keller, Ernest Hemingway, Thomas Mann and Albert Einstein.

Book burning is not something limited to the Holocaust, the Spanish Inquisition and antiquity. Just last year, a preacher from Gainesville, Florida publicly burned a copy of the Qu'ran, despite a direct plea from President Obama to refrain from such a hateful act of religious intolerance.

And in 2010, a group of university students in India burned copies of *Such a Long Journey*—a beautiful novel by the way—which was written by Indo-Canadian novelist Rohinton Mistry and which won the Governor General's Literary Award in 1991. These same students intimidated the University of Mumbai into dropping the book from the syllabus. Why? The leader of the book burners complained of "obscene and vulgar language" in the novel and of negative references to India's nationalist politicians.

I happen to love Rohinton Mistry's novels—especially *A Fine Balance*, which I feel bears a spiritual resemblance to *The Book of Negroes*. Although we have never had a proper conversation, I felt an additional kinship to Rohinton Mistry when I learned that his writing, too, had been burned overseas.

Perhaps Rohinton Mistry and I should form a club. After all, writers form all sorts of associations. Once I had lunch in Calgary with three other novelists and we were all whining about nasty literary reviews that we had endured. I thought that my story of an unfavourable review in an Edmonton newspaper would impress my lunchmates, but my late friend Paul Quarrington took the top prize. One of his novels had earned, in one newspaper, this critical headline: "Trashy Book Waste of Paper." So if writers bond to talk business, or to oppose the incarceration of our peers, or to argue for better royalties for our e-books, perhaps we should also be gathering to form a support group for those who have had their books burned.

Let me return to a more serious note. Some friends and family members were surprised to see how much Mr. Groenberg's email upset me. And I was surprised myself. Earlier in my career, when very few people had heard of my books, I sometimes joked with friends that all I needed was to be the subject of a book censorship campaign. That, for sure, would increase my sales! I supposed that a few writers whose books are banned, censored or burned end up gaining a few extra sales, but many of them face the more likely possibly of seeing publishers, bookstores and others back away. Who wants to be associated with a writer who will cause trouble, or stir controversy, or attract vigorous public criticism?

I have a troubled relationship with my book burners in Amsterdam.

One emotional challenge for me, in dealing with the issue, was that the Dutch book burners, albeit small in number, were people of Surinamese descent. Suriname, in South America, was one of the most important slave colonies of the Dutch. In the broader Diaspora of African peoples, these are my own people. And it hurts, frankly, when your own people reject you, or tell you that you don't belong, or challenge the very identity that you have shaped for yourself. I don't agree with those who burned my book. But I empathize with them. And that, and the troubling relationship we have with books that offend us deeply, is what I want to talk about.

I am not merely a reader and writer with an obvious bias in favour of the freedom to read and write. I am also a parent of five children, and the son of a woman and a man who devoted much of their lives to advancing the cause of human rights in Canada.

My late father, Daniel G. Hill, was an African American born in Independence, Missouri in 1923. He served as a soldier in the highly segregated American Army in World War II. Up to the end of that war, he was reminded most days of his life that he was a black man with second-class rights as an American citizen. Good enough to die for his country, but not good enough to eat in restaurants with white people, drink from their water fountains, swim in their pools or, for that matter, fall in love with one of their daughters.

My mother, Donna Hill, was a White American born in 1928 in South Dakota but raised in Oak Park, Illinois. She navigated the miraculous, early life transition of leaving behind her conservative family roots to become a civil rights activist.

After my parents met and fell in love in one of the only two racially integrated housing co-ops in Washington, DC in 1952, they married and the next day left the USA forever. They moved to Toronto, where my mother continued her work in social activism and my father began his PHD studies in sociology at the University of Toronto.

Yes, I am the child of two sociologists. Consider me a survivor. What else is there but emotional survival, when one's father catches one pummelling one's brother, pulls out a scholarly book by French sociologist Émile Durkheim, points a finger and calls out "Deviant Behaviour"?

My father didn't have much time for children exhibiting deviant behaviour. He was busy finishing his PHD thesis, circa 1960, called "Negroes in Toronto: A Sociological Study" and a few years later he was busy creating the Ontario Human Rights Commission—the first commission of its kind in Canada. Human rights, Black history in Canada, the stories of slavery, the end of slavery, and the civil rights movements in this country and in the USA formed part of our kitchen table talk at home in Don Mills—a sleepy, affluent, overwhelmingly white suburb of Toronto.

My father is no longer around to answer my detailed questions, but I remember him telling me that when I was very young, he argued against the use of racist books and textbooks in the public schools of Ontario. He was sensitive to outrageous descriptions and depictions of Black people—and other racial minorities—in literature, and, by the time he was hitting his full stride as young professional in the 1960s and 1970s, felt fully ready to do battle with them.

One of the books that most outraged him was *Little Black Sambo*. For those of you who don't know, *Little Black Sambo* is a children's book written by Helen Bannerman and first published in 1899.

The original character appears as a boy from India, but over time the character, in North America especially, is seen to be black. Sambo, like Aunt Jemima, is a catch-all, hurtful name meant to refer to Black people who are in a subjugated, menial, servile position. Sambo evokes the image of the North American slave who is satisfied with his state of servitude.

In this famous children's story, Sambo surrenders his fancy clothes to four tigers so they will not eat him. The vain tigers chase each other around a tree and melt into a pool of butter. Sambo recovers his clothes and his mother, whose name is Black Mumbo, uses the butter to make 169 pancakes. Black Sambo eats them all. The depiction of the character "Little Black Sambo" falls into the camp of "pickaninny" stereotyping that offends many African Canadian and African American readers. Black Sambo has every stereotype going: bare feet, flashy clothes, exaggerated facial features and gluttony to boot. If that does not suffice, he sports the name of the servile, satisfied slave, of William Thackeray's black-skinned Indian servant from his 1847 novel *Vanity Fair*.

I don't remember if my father called for the book to be yanked from Ontario schools. I asked his lifelong friend and confidant, Alan Borovoy—now retired, but the former general counsel for the Canadian Civil Liberties Association—but he couldn't remember either exactly what battle my father might have fought on that front. I asked Alan—a vigorous defender of free speech, even on unpopular fronts such as arguing that disseminators of hate literature should not be prosecuted in Canada—and he answered that it was one thing to try to ban a book completely in society, and less aggressive to argue that a school or school board should not be giving its imprimatur to racist literature.

But this is where we fall into very tricky territory. Half the world, it seems, wants to pull one book or another off school shelves, because the children just aren't ready for it. On the one hand, you have your basic left wingers like my father and me, who would be scandalized to think that a teacher in the year 2012 would want to have Grade 1 kids reading *Little Black Sambo*. On the other hand, you have your right wing and fundamentalist groups that object to the children's book *And Tango Makes Three*, the true story of two gay penguins raising a baby penguin in New York's Central Park Zoo.

Just imagine. If the leftwingers and the rightwingers formed a coalition, they could yank half the books out of the

Canadian school curriculum. Together, they could ensure that no school or public library book would ever be allowed to provoke, disturb, challenge, offend or outrage another reader for the rest of time. They could control our minds forever after. In the publicly funded shelves of schools and libraries, the only thing we would have left is *Anne of Green Gables*.

I think I can dispense of two matters immediately. I wouldn't want any book in a library or bookstore banned, pulled, removed or burned. Period. We can hate them, dissect them, learn from them or praise them, but we need to leave books alone and let readers come to terms with them. We can teach young people to be aware and to be critical thinkers. But to believe that we can protect young people from the ideas in literature is self-delusional, in the extreme. In today's electronic age, dissidents who are prosecuted and persecuted in a country such as China are more likely to be bloggers than novelists. Still, even in the year 2012, the book holds a special place in the world of argument. To those who would ban them and to those who would defend them, books remain symbols of ideas, defiance, originality and individuality—loved by some for the very same reasons that they are despised by others.

From a practical standpoint, book censorship seems ludicrous. You can find all manner of violence, hate, pornography and filth on the Internet, and on television, and in film. We don't seem to get too exercised about that. Many or most young people in Canada have access to the Net and to television, and a great many of them have unrestricted access. Between the Net and television and film, there is something in the palette of colours to meet virtually every definition of gross, and to offend virtually every person on the planet. But heaven forbid that our children read a book about gay penguins in the Central Park Zoo! It seems misplaced and unfair to single out literature for the loudest complaints about allegedly offensive ideas.

Now, let's consider the thornier problem of grossly hateful or offensive material in the schools. What do we do about it?

Is there such a thing as free speech? Not really. You are not allowed to stand on a street corner in Canada and incite people to violence. It is—rightly, in my opinion—against the Criminal Code of Canada to disseminate hate literature in this country. Clearly, there is room for only so many books in a Grade 3 classroom, or on a Grade 11 English curriculum, or in a school library for that matter. Somebody has to decide which books should be bought, made available to students in libraries, and taught. And it is only normal that a range of societal values will influence the decisions of those who are buying books for students, and teaching children in the classroom.

I openly admit that in the neighbourhood of Hamilton where I live with my wife and children, I would be appalled if I found a Grade 1 teacher reading racist literature to his or her six-year-old charges. I'm sure I would have some questions to ask. I would make sure to speak to my own children—although mine are now well past that age—about the book, and its bias, and its limitations in my view. This is my right as a parent. But, unless the book violated our hate laws or some other Canadian law, I don't believe that I could argue that it should be removed entirely from the school library, or made inaccessible to children who wanted to read it. I think the hypocrisy of saying "I can read this and handle it but others must be protected from it" applies to children too.

Books are expressions of human thought. It is fair to criticize them, even virulently. But I just don't think we should be burning or banning them or choosing to make them inaccessible.

Anyway, I can't really argue to pull a book I happen to hate from the shelves, because it would then be impossible for me to defend other books against attacks led by other people.

I have already waded into two public fights over the use of books in the schools of Ontario. In one case, about 15 years ago, a group of people in the Halton District School Board banded together under the rather unbelievable acronym PACT. This stands for Parents Against Corrupt Teachers. PACT formed in Halton to do battle against *Foxfire*, a novel by the American literary icon Joyce Carol Oates. Oates is one of the most famous, prolific and respected literary novelists in the USA. Her novel, which I have read closely, is about the troubling dynamics of an extremely violent gang of impoverished, abused teenage girls in upper New York State in the middle of the 20th century.

Foxfire features teenage girls who have been abused and mistreated, and who then form a gang to mete out punishments against those who have hurt them. The girls end up meting out far more severe punishments than they have received. And their language is not pretty. There is much dialogue, and suffice it to say that they do not sound like nuns. The members of Parents Against Corrupt Teachers actually assembled a compendium of every single four-letter word in the book. This word appears on line four of Page 1. That word appears on line 18 of Page 2. Etc. It is a long and boring list. And it is entirely beside the point. Still, the group created enough of a fuss to lead the school board to temporarily remove the book from a high school reading list until the matter could be considered further. Personally, I fail to see the need to protect 17-year-old readers from the very language they use, with some dexterity, on the street.

A self-mocking note here. In my own home, I have a hyperliterate, book-devouring 15-year-old stepdaughter named Eve Freedman who has a mouth like a soldier. This is the same child who, five years ago, helped me come up with an alternate American title for my novel. These days, I don't know what to do about all her swearing. She is a bright kid. She has surely read more books, in her short 15 years, than I have read in my entire lifetime. My wife, although she flinched, had pretty well given up on Eve's potty mouth and was hoping that she might exit from this phase by her 16th birthday. Fat chance. I came up with an idea. It seems to be working. And it goes like this. Eve is not allowed to swear on the first floor of our house. On the second floor—in her bedroom, for example, or in the bathroom—she may have at it. But no swearing on the main floor—not in the kitchen, dining room, living room or in the hall by the front

door. Occasionally, she tests me by putting both feet on the
first step leading upstairs and letting rip with some foul
obscenity. She is immune, on the first step. But she only
tried that once or twice, to see if I would honour my end of
the bargain. By limiting her potty mouth to the second floor,
we pretty well got her to cut out 95% of it. The remainder of
her swearing hardly matters, because when she is upstairs
she generally closes the door to her bedroom, where we can't
hear her.

To me, it is entirely laughable that Eve Freedman, Queen
of the Hamilton Potty Mouths, would be scandalized by a
few hundred choice swear words in *Foxfire*. But even a Girl
Guide or Boy Scout who is never allowed curse at home will
not see their universe upended by reading Joyce Carol Oates.
Foxfire happens to be a very good novel. For those who care
to read it attentively, it contains a warning to those who
would allow their minds to be overtaken by a gang—any
gang at all.

Eve joined me in the second public fight. It had to do
with the use of *Three Wishes: Palestinian and Israeli Children
Speak*, by the Canadian writer Deborah Ellis. *Three Wishes*
is a work of non-fiction for children. It contains the real
monologues in the voices of real children—some Jewish,
others Palestinian—who are caught up in the tensions and
hatred of living in what is essentially a war zone. Some of
the children express fear and hatred of the other. Many lack
opportunities to get to know children on the other side of
the divide. One of the children interviewed was the sibling
of a suicide bomber. This inflamed the Canadian Jewish

Congress, and the next thing you knew this incredibly thoughtful and insightful book—in the voices of children, about their very lives as children in the Middle East—was removed from the hands of children in the Toronto District School Board. Apparently, Palestinian and Israeli children are old enough to live through hell, but children in Canada are not old enough to read about it.

Eve went to bat in favour of this book, speaking—as I did—at a Toronto press conference in its defence. It was interesting to note that in the uproar over whether the book was appropriate to be read by children in school, nobody had thought to ask the opinions of children. Eve adored the books of Deborah Ellis, and she was outraged by the decision to remove the book from a special school reading program, and this provided the impetus for her articulate defence of the book. As a result, at the age of ten, Eve became the first child in Canada to win the Freedom to Read Award.

Eve does not just own an uncensored potty mouth—it is an award-winning mouth that can be put to intelligent and passionate argument.

I have a bizarre little anecdote about book censorship. There are thousands of stories, but this one is just too good to pass up. I got it from Pearce Carefoote's book, *Forbidden Fruit*.

The Naked and the Dead, the first novel by American Norman Mailer, was published in 1946. It offered a frank, brutal and utterly unsentimental portrait of the American army in the South Pacific in World War II. It was a massive bestseller, although the *Globe and Mail* described it as "pure

pornography." In 1949, it was banned from Canada's bookstores and libraries by the Canadian Minister of National
Revenue, J. J. McCann, who had jurisdiction over the impor-
tation of foreign literature. The minister admitted that he
had never read the book, but based his judgement on the
highlighted "bits" his advisors had deemed salacious.

I have one other anecdote to share. I am excerpting this
detail from the 2011 "Freedom to Read" publication released
by the Book and Periodical Council.

In 1923, the commissioner of the Department of Customs
and Excise directed officers at the border to ban the novel
Ulysses, by James Joyce, from entering Canada. He regarded
the novel as obscene and illegal. At the time, no one had the
right to appeal a Customs ruling to a court. A banned publication stayed on the prohibited list until Customs officials
changed their minds. Some 26 years later, in 1949, David
Dim, the deputy minister of the Department of Customs
and Excise, read *Ulysses* while he was on vacation and decided
that it was no longer obscene. Without fanfare, Sim lifted
the ban and allowed the novel into Canada.

Let me reassure you that 1923 and 1949 were not the last
times that provocative books were prevented from entering
Canada. Books—including gay-themed books—continue to
be held up regularly at the border.

Books continue to come under fire annually. According
to the Book and Periodical Council, some of the many writers
of fiction to face challenges of book bans and censorship in
Canada include Mordecai Richler, Anthony Burgess,
Stephen King, Margaret Atwood, D. H. Lawrence, Alice

Munro, John Steinbeck, Salman Rushdie, Charlaine Harris, Timothy Findley and Jane Rule. That is just a short sample from a much longer list.

Observing the inherent elitism in the decision by authority figures to protect the masses from troublesome literature, Carefoote cites a particularly effective quote from the author Charles Rembar: "I never heard a prosecutor or a condemning judge announce that *his* moral fibre had been injured by the book in question. It was always someone else's moral fibre for which anxiety was felt."

Let's return to Amsterdam. It was personally troubling to see a segment of the very community that I would hope to court and connect with—people of Surinamese descent in The Netherlands—rising up against my own book. To come to terms with the book cover burning, I want to meditate for a moment on my own relationship to The Netherlands and on what I have come to know about its own treatment of people of African descent.

I have a long-standing connection with Dutch people and with The Netherlands. In 1974, at the age of 17, I took off to Europe for the summer with my best friend—a Canadian of Dutch ancestry by the name of Jack Veugelers—who later became a sociologist! We stayed with various members of his extended family—all very kind aunts, uncles and grandparents—for about a month. I have since visited a number of times, to give readings, to run in a half marathon in Amsterdam as a fundraiser for the Canadian Diabetes Association, and in 2011, to give readings and interviews to help launch the Dutch edition of my novel, *The Book of Negroes*.

Friends, publishers, media and strangers have always treated me kindly in The Netherlands. I enjoy the country, and have made friends with many Dutch people. Please keep that in mind as I tell this bizarre story.

Canadians and the Dutch have one unusual point in common. We both tend to deny, or sweep under the rug, the history of slavery as carried out by our own countries. Slavery was practiced in Eastern Canada—modern day Ontario, Québec, New Brunswick, Nova Scotia and even PEI—until it was finally abolished throughout most of the British empire in 1834. We don't generally like to talk about that, and would far prefer to point an accusatory moral finger at Americans for their own history of slavery, or at South Africans for their own history of Apartheid. I wrote *The Book of Negroes* to document a difficult and little known story of the Black Loyalists of Nova Scotia. As I have mentioned earlier, I gave the novel its name to resurrect a British naval ledger documenting the exodus of 3,000 blacks who fled Manhattan at the end of the American Revolution and came to Nova Scotia to insist on their freedom, and to cash in on the promises of the British who had offered them security and freedom in exchange for service during the American Revolutionary War.

When the novel came out in 2011 in The Netherlands, my Dutch publisher translated the title directly from *The Book of Negroes*. It was called *Het Negerboek*.

Just as Canada has its history of slavery that some in this country have ignored, The Netherlands has its own slave history.

Holland did not abolish slavery until 1863, the same year as Abraham Lincoln's Emancipation Proclamation.

While on book tour in The Netherlands last year, I visited the Middelburg Zeeland Archives in the small town of Middelburg in the south of Holland. There, I thumbed through the original records of slave ships run by the Middelburg Commercial Company. In the 18th and 19th centuries, that one company alone sold thousands of Africans into slavery in the former Dutch colony of Suriname.

During the five years I had spent researching *The Book of Negroes*, I had never held in my hands the actual, original records of a company that shipped slaves. But I did so in Middelburg, and came across numerous stark and painful details. Between about 1730 and the end of the Dutch slavery period, The Middelburg Commercial Company made 113 slave ship journeys to Africa. The company described its human cargo with the following, disgusting term: "curly cattle." There were many blatant references to the company's sales of human beings. For example, the company's ship *Gertrude and Christina*, which arrived in Paramaibo, Suriname on October 6, 1775, describes some of its property in this way:

"Female Negro healthy with some fire in her eyes," sold for 130 guilders
"Negro boy healthy with umbilical hernia skinny," sold for 115 guilders

I won't go on. Suffice it to say that it was a painful time in Dutch and African history, and that the legacy of this injustice lingers—and festers—in The Netherlands today. The Turkish scholar Jan Erk, who teaches at the University of Leiden in the Netherlands, notes that the four biggest immigrant communities in the Netherlands are Turks, Moroccans, Antilleans and Surinamese. Together, they total almost one million people in a country of 17 million. Nonetheless, Geert Wilders, an important and influential politician in the country, has gained popularity and political currency by leading a political party that spews anti-Islamic rhetoric. As Jan Erk pointed out last year in an article entitled "The Famous Dutch (In)Tolerance" for *Current History*, in one media interview Wilders derided Islam by calling it—and I quote—a "violent and retarded" religion.

Some Blacks, North Africans and Muslims in The Netherlands feel under siege these days. There are two references to Black people in contemporary Dutch culture that seem to be particularly offensive to people of Surinamese and other Black descent living in The Netherlands today. I want to mention them, because they contextualize the response of Mr. Groenberg in deciding to burn my book cover last year.

You have all heard of Saint Nicholas. In the Netherlands, December 5 is set aside as the day to celebrate the birthday of Sinterklaas, as he is known there. He has a Black helper—a white man who is dressed up in blackface and shown to have exaggerated black features such as thick red lips and a wild mop of an Afro—who goes by the name of Zwarte Piet, or Black Peter. On the day of the annual Sinterklaas parade, Black Peter traditionally cavorts around in pantaloons like a fool and a bumpkin. In some instances, he dispenses candy to good children. In other instances, he carries a rod for punishment and a burlap sack into which unruly children will be stuffed and carted back to Spain, where he and Saint Nick come from.

I asked Amy Abdou, who at the time of the book cover burning incident worked in Amsterdam for the now-defunct National Institute for the Study of Dutch Slavery and its Legacy, to interpret Zwarte Piet to me. Zwarte Piet, she told me, emerges after a time when the Dutch parliament was discussing ways to abolish slavery and yet keep the enslaved Africans working on the plantations. At the time of abolition in 1863 in the Dutch colonies, those who had been enslaved were not truly liberated. They were forced into a sort of reintegration program that led to ten more years of indentured servitude.

Ms. Abdou goes on to explain that out of this story emerges Zwarte Piet, an enslaved man who is so grateful to his "liberators" that he remains forever in their servitude. The costume that Piet wears in the Sinterklaas celebrations comes directly from the page-like outfits enslaved Africans were forced to wear in the 19th century, when they were brought to Europe to serve their masters in their homes. There are several images of these "pages" in Dutch paintings of this time, often seen with eyes cast down, helping to dress a wealthy man or woman.

Ms. Abdou notes that Zwarte Piet inherited many of the same characteristics of the so-called "darky iconography" of the late 19th–early 20th century: thick lips, Afro wig, a perpetual look of surprise and stupidity. The tradition of wearing blackface to portray Zwarte Piet is most likely an early 20th century invention, following the popularity of minstrel shows in America and possibly tied to an older tradition of men darkening their faces to portray the devil and chasing children to scare them into behaving well. Up until the 1960s, Zwarte Piet played the foil to Saint Nicholas's wisdom and goodness. He was the one who doled out punishment with a switch and carried bad children back to Spain in a bag. During the 1970s and 80s, white Dutch who portrayed Zwarte Piet would often assume a Surinamese or Caribbean accent.

To this day, we still see Black Peter cavorting around in his stereotypical manner in the annual Sinterklaas celebrations, and you can imagine how offensive this is to many Blacks—from the Netherlands and elsewhere—who have to put up with it. Perhaps it will change over time. Last year, the annual Sinterklaas celebration in New Westminster, BC was cancelled over objections to the depiction to Black Peter.

Doubtless, many participants—Dutch and Canadians alike—in the Sinterklaas celebrations have no idea of the offence they are causing to people of African descent. They may well not know of the complicated nature of this cultural celebration. To them, it is simply good fun.

There is one more stunning reference to Blacks in contemporary Dutch culture that ties into the burning of my book cover by some in the Dutch Surinamese community. But before I go there, I want to say that many Western nations offer up stereotypical or disturbing images of

Blacks. When I was growing up in Don Mills, Ontario in the 1960s, my mother and father barred the use of any Aunt Jemima products from our household because of the obvious racial stereotyping of the black domestic slave who is ever so happy, day in and day out, to cook up great meals for the people who own her. So we, in Canada, are fully as guilty of racial stereotyping as the Dutch.

But I'm going to speak about the Dutch now, because they are the ones who burned my book cover.

As I learned when I first travelled in The Netherlands at the age of 17, the Dutch have a thing about chocolates and sweet treats. They even sprinkle bits of chocolate on their bread in the morning. One of the most popular sweets in The Netherlands is akin to a chocolate-covered marshmallow. Traditionally, these chocolates have been called Negerzoenen. That translates as "Negro Kisses." Historically, old advertising for these chocolates is blatantly racist and trades openly on the most brazen and offensive racial stereotypes. In one advertisement, a domineering black woman with huge breasts shrieks at a cowering white man: "Don't you like my kisses?" I could go on and on about these advertisements, but you can see them for yourself if you google "Negerzoenen."

There is an understandable sensitivity among some people in The Netherlands to a history of racism carried out in their country and elsewhere in the world. As noted in detail in a book by the writer Rebecca Knuth, on January 19, 1984, some 50 protesters belonging to a group called Amsterdammers Against Racism and Discrimination

stormed into the South African Institute and attempted to
destroy its vast collection of 22,000 rare books and archival
documents—some dating back to the 16th century—related
to the history and literature of South Africa. They sprayed
some rare documents with tar and paint and threw others
into the street and into an adjacent canal. Hundreds of rare,
irreplaceable books were destroyed or forever lost. Although
the library had been used by many scholars who were critical
of the South African regime, the protestors told a journalist
later that they "wanted to undertake a symbolic action
against repressive ideas, against an organization which
makes propaganda for a fascist and murdering regime..."
In *Burning Books and Leveling Libraries: Extremist Violence and
Cultural Destruction*, Knuth notes that the political cause
of the protestors was largely lost on the media and on the
public at large, which roundly condemned the attack on the
library.[3]

And this brings us back to the book cover burning.
Although I completely condemn the attempt to silence
and intimidate my publisher and me, I feel the healthiest
response is to engage with the ideas of the person behind
the incident.

Roy Groenberg, the man who wrote to me to threaten
that he would burn my book and who then went on to burn
the cover for the benefit of rolling TV cameras, recently led a
campaign that was ultimately successful to persuade Buys,
the manufacturer of the offensive chocolate, to change the
name of the chocolate. I applaud Mr. Groenberg for fighting
that fight. In other circumstances, I would have stood

beside him and agreed with the need to change the name of those chocolates. Unfortunately for me, if you google "Negerzoenen" you will also find my face and the cover of the Dutch edition of my novel.

I understand that Roy Groenberg and his followers are offended by my title, even though he openly states that he has not read the book and will not do so under its current title. And I understand, especially with the history of slavery and the ongoing manifestations of racial disrespect in Holland, why Mr. Groenberg and his followers would react so explosively to the title of my book. They are entitled to their reactions. I know where they are coming from. In some respects they are coming from the same place as my father who, some 50 years ago, objected to the use of racist literature in Ontario schools.

Racial terminology will always fail, because it is absurd to try to define a person by race. In North America we have witnessed a kaleidoscopic evolution of racial terminology over the last 50 years. Although my father proudly called himself a Negro for most of his life, you can be sure that he would not be using the term today, if he were alive. And our own grandchildren will surely laugh at the terms currently in use, such as Black and African Canadian. When they are running the country, they'll bring their own terms into play. I like to imagine what people will be saying, instead of "Negro," "Black" or "African Canadian," in 50 years and how they will scorn today's terminology.

I tell my own children that no single word is entirely out of bounds. One must simply know the heft of each word, and use it appropriately. If that means employing discretion around archaic or racist terms, so be it. I don't use "Negro" in day-to-day language. To this day, I still cringe at the sound of "Nigger" or "Nigga" in hip hop lyrics. But there is sometimes room to use painful language to reclaim our own history.

In other circumstances, if Mr. Groenberg had come to me or to my publisher before the book appeared, and had asked to have a conversation about the title, I would have heard him out. If I had become convinced that the title might profoundly offend a number of Surinamese Dutch, I might well have argued for the use of a different title. If Mr. Groenberg had asked me to attend a public meeting to discuss the title in detail, I would have done so. At least we would have had a chance to discuss the matter, and I would have explained the historical roots of the title. I don't agree with his methods, but I suspect that on nine issues out of ten with respect to the history and current situation of peoples of the African Diaspora, we are on the same page.

The problem, however, is that burning books aims to intimidate writers, readers, publishers and booksellers, and to stifle dialogue. A book burner is not itching for discussion. A book burner has a match to light, and now!

The very purpose of literature is to enlighten, disturb, awaken and provoke. Literature should get us talking—even when we disagree. Literature should bring us into the same room—not over matches, but over coffee and conversation. It should inspire recognition of our mutual humanity. Together.

I can't see any good coming out of burning or banning books.

Let's talk, instead.

Notes

1. Lawrence Hill, *Some Great Thing* (Toronto: HarperCollins Canada, 2009), P.S. 10.

2. Pearce J. Carefoot, *Forbidden Fruit: Banned, Censored, and Challenged Books from Dante to Harry Potter* (Toronto: Lester, Mason, Begg, 2007).

3. Rebecca Knuth, *Burning Books and Leveling Libraries: Extremist Violence and Cultural Destruction* (Westport, CT: Praeger, 2006), 64.